ANGKOR WAT: Carvings at Prasat Bayon temple, Cambodia.

LOST CITIES

GILES LAROCHE

HOUGHTON MIFFLIN HARCOURT
BOSTON   NEW YORK

KARNAK: Avenue of
Sphinxes, Egypt.

TO CRAIG

hmhbooks.com

Manufactured in Malaysia
TWP 10 9 8 7 6 5 4 3 2 1
4500786539

Copyright © 2020 by Giles Laroche

Book design by Cara Llewellyn.
The display type was set in 1786 GLC Fournier.
The text type was set in Sabon and Stone Sans.
The cut-paper relief illustrations were created with
a variety of hand-painted papers.

Library of Congress Control Number: 2018052168
ISBN: 978-1-328-75364-9

INTRODUCTION

On mountaintops or islands, in deserts, along the banks of rivers or near the sea, ancient cities once thrived. Some were part of vast empires, while others were small and independent. Many lasted for centuries, even millennia, and went through great transformations. Most ultimately didn't survive, but clues to their past exist in the ruins of their buildings and monuments.

Who were the people that lived in these places? Why did they build their structures in the ways they did? Why were the cities lost—and how were they found?

Each of these cultures made important contributions to the evolution of civilization: they invented the wheel, the alphabet, the first plumbing system, various forms of government, works of art and monumental architecture, and methods of building still used today. Many contain mysteries of construction and purpose we are still trying to solve. For example, how were such massive stones moved to construct the temples and pyramids of Egypt? Why were the stone figures of Easter Island erected?

Today, are there lost cities still waiting to be found? And thousands of years from now, what will *our* cities and monuments look like to people living then?

KARNAK TEMPLE

If you lived here thousands of years ago, your family might have thronged with other people into this Egyptian city to worship the sun god Amun at the complex of temples called Karnak, built by pharaohs to honor their King of Gods. You would have passed along avenues lined with hundreds of stone sculptures depicting Amun as a sphinx (a creature with a lion's body and a ram's head) before entering the first temple, with its rows of towering columns carved with hieroglyphs, symbols that tell stories about the gods and pharaohs depicted in the wall paintings. Here you would have requested Amun to bestow good health, happiness, and prosperity upon you and your family in the present, as well as in the afterlife in which all Egyptians believed.

LOCATION: Karnak,* part of Thebes, a city in Luxor, Upper Egypt

WHO LIVED HERE? First settled around 5000 BCE, the Egyptian civilization had unified a vast area along the Nile River by 3100 BCE and was to last over three thousand years, longer than any other in antiquity. For centuries Karnak was the world's largest religious center, and thousands of citizens were servants or slaves to the ruling kings or queens, who were called pharaohs. Egyptians developed a pictorial language, called hieroglyphs, written on paper made of papyrus leaves, and invented surgical tools and monumental forms of architecture, such as the famous pyramids.

WHY WAS IT LOST? Assyrian invasions around 670 BCE damaged many monuments and displaced the people, who moved to other Egyptian cities. When the Roman emperor Constantine adopted Christianity and visited a desolate Karnak, he ordered the closing of all remaining pagan (non-Christian) temples.

HOW WAS IT FOUND? Karnak, more than five hundred miles down the Nile, remained largely unknown until 1859, when a Venetian traveler wrote about the temple complex.

WHAT'S MYSTERIOUS? The god Amun, who was known as "the hidden one," was believed to die at sunset only to become reborn each day with the rising sun. His face is usually painted blue. Was this done to make him invisible, even during the day?

*All names throughout these pages are pronounced phonetically unless otherwise indicated.

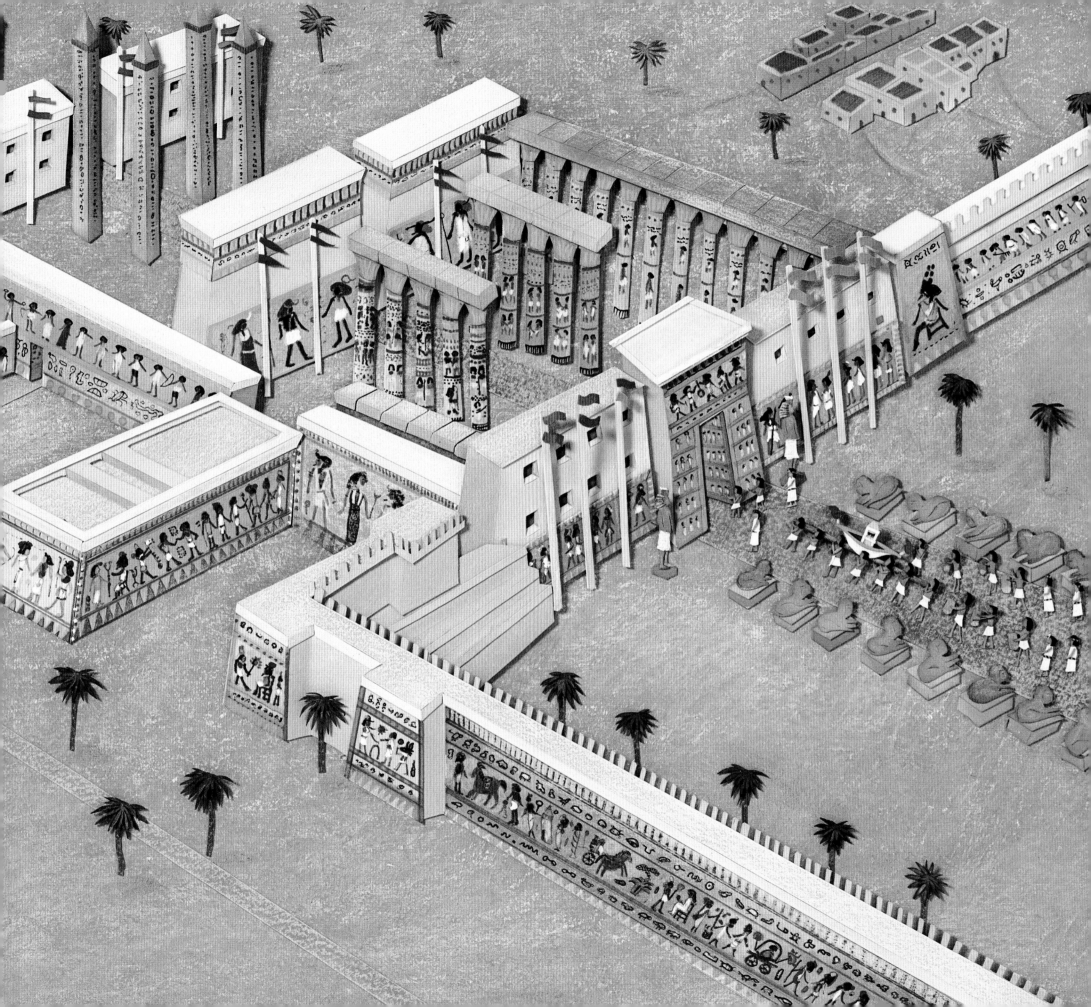

BABYLON

If you had entered this fabled city during the reign of the ruler Hammurabi, you would have passed through a high, guarded gate dedicated to the goddess Ishtar. Then you could have climbed to the top of a ziggurat temple for a bird's-eye view of the city and one of the seven wonders of the world—the Hanging Gardens of Babylon.

LOCATION: Babylon, once the world's largest city, was the capital of Mesopotamia, in what is now Iraq.

WHO LIVED HERE? Founded around 2350 BCE as a small village on the Euphrates River, Babylon grew and thrived for more than two thousand years. Cursive writing, the recording of history on clay tablets, irrigation, the wheel, and advances in architecture, such as the ziggurat (a type of stepped tower), were some of the Mesopotamians' innovative achievements. But the most famous was probably the Code of Hammurabi, a set of governing laws that kept order among the citizens of a country.

WHY WAS IT LOST? After Alexander the Great of Greece conquered Babylon in 331 BCE, the city slowly declined until its buildings were in ruins, buried in the desert sands.

HOW WAS IT FOUND? Babylon was lost, but not forgotten, living on in stories and legends. In 1899, two thousand years after its abandonment, an archaeologist unearthed the location of the ziggurat and the ruins of Ishtar Gate. Babylon was found.

WHAT'S MYSTERIOUS? Water was scarce in Babylon, so how were the Hanging Gardens irrigated? The only known ruins of an aqueduct (a bridge-like structure that carries water) have been found in the nearby city of Nineveh, but not in Babylon; so the water source for the gardens remains a mystery.

AKROTIRI ON THE ISLAND OF THERA

If you had lived in the island village of Akrotiri, you might have sailed on a boat to nearby islands to sell and buy pottery, metal tools, clothing, and even a pet blue monkey. Your three-story house on the slope of the island's volcanic mountain would have been filled with furniture and pottery made by family and friends, and the rooms decorated with frescoes (wall paintings) by local artists.

LOCATION: On the island of Thera, in the Aegean Sea, Greece

WHO LIVED HERE? Under the Minoans, ancestors of the ancient Greeks, Thera became an important stopping point on the sailing route between the islands of Crete and Cyprus. Minoans were skilled artists, had a written language, and their kings, unlike the Babylonian and Egyptian rulers, shared their wealth with Akrotiri's citizens. They were also among the first people to have running water for their homes—both hot and cold.

WHY WAS IT LOST? What was once the high mountain on this island is today a deep harbor where ships anchor. How did this happen? After flourishing for five hundred years, the Minoan civilization on Thera abruptly ended in 1627 BCE when the mountain exploded in one of the largest volcanic eruptions in recorded

history. The center of the island became a water-filled crater and the nearby town of Akrotiri was buried in ash.

HOW WAS IT FOUND? In 1967, after a century of ongoing archaeological excavations, Akrotiri, and its houses with painted frescoes, was finally uncovered. The fact that few personal objects have been found suggests the inhabitants were given advance warning of the eruption and fortunately escaped.

WHAT'S MYSTERIOUS? Many scholars believe the eruption of Thera inspired the famous Greek philosopher Plato to write of the mysterious lost world of Atlantis. Others claim Plato's Atlantis existed elsewhere, in many different locations around the globe. Who is right?

HERCULANEUM

If you were a young Roman living in Herculaneum, you could go hiking in the nearby mountains or fishing and swimming in the Mediterranean. Here you would watch colorful boats arriving from distant ports, laden with exotic goods, such as woven carpets, amphoras (tall earthen jars) filled with olive oil, and animals brought from Africa, including lions and ostriches. Then you might attend a performance in the amphitheater, an outdoor, semicircular theater with tiered seating facing the stage.

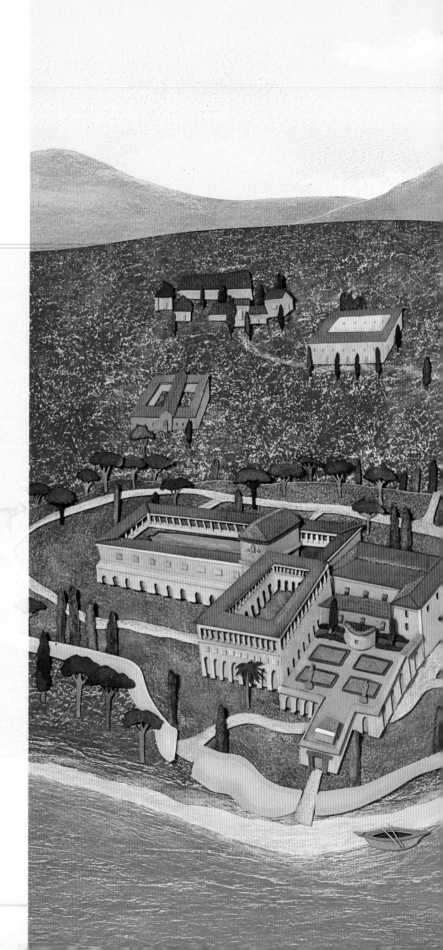

LOCATION: Campania region of Italy, south of modern-day Naples

WHO LIVED HERE? First settled in the sixth century BCE by Samnite tribes, Herculaneum was later occupied by the Greeks who named it after their mythical hero Hercules. In 89 BCE it was conquered by the Romans, becoming part of one of the most advanced cultures and largest empires in the ancient world. Roman engineers and architects invented the dome and developed a lengthy system of paved roads, just two of their many advancements that transformed the way we build and live.

WHY WAS IT LOST? During the summer of 79 CE, the ground shook and rumbled as Mount Vesuvius, towering above Herculaneum, sent out ominous clouds of smoke that darkened the sky—even on the brightest of days. Then Vesuvius abruptly erupted, and within minutes covered Herculaneum and the nearby town of Pompeii and their people with an overwhelming flow of ash, pumice stone, and gases streaming down from the volcano.

HOW WAS IT FOUND? For almost 1,700 years the city was lost, buried under one hundred feet of volcanic ash that destroyed the life of the city, but preserved Herculaneum's houses and villas, including furniture, Roman bronze sculptures, and even the skeletons of those unable to escape. In 1750 workers digging a well above Herculaneum struck the marble pavement of a Roman amphitheater, awakening the city from its long slumber before an incredulous world.

WHAT'S MYSTERIOUS? Hundreds of papyrus scrolls, perfectly preserved, have been found in the library of an enormous, nearly intact buried villa (at right). They are currently being scanned by modern infrared technology. Will these scrolls reveal ancient, valuable secrets about life in Herculaneum and the history of the Roman Empire?

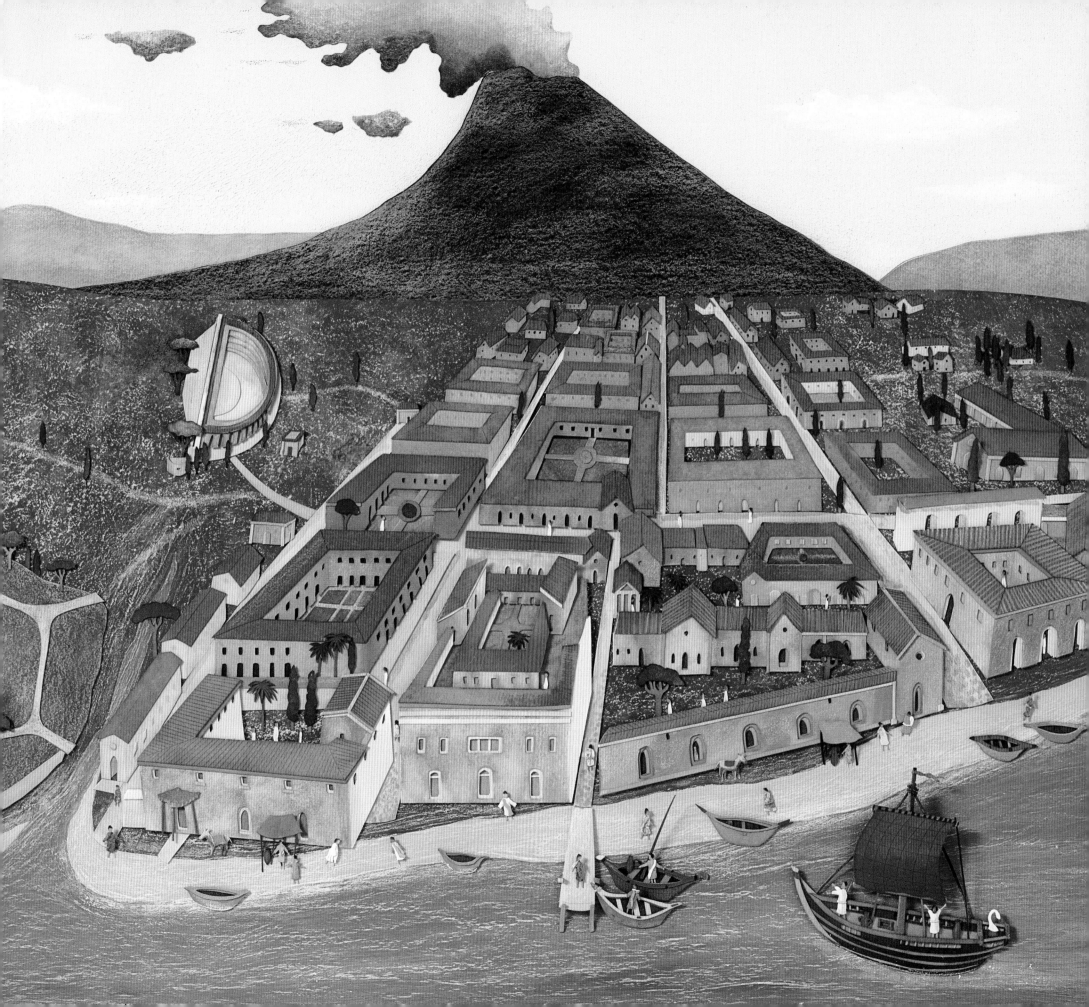

GREAT ZIMBABWE

What would it be like to live in a village made entirely of stone and surrounded by towering walls as tall as trees, topped with soapstone statues of birds with human features? Once inside these walls you would find houses for the common people and the kings and a mysterious thirty-foot-tall solid stone tower. If you climbed these walls, you might see rhinos and herds of giraffes, a strolling lion, or a cheetah running swiftly over the vast savanna. Inside the walls, your family and friends would greet traders from afar, with whom you would exchange items of iron or gold made in Great Zimbabwe for foreign goods, such as ceramics and glass beads, rare fabrics and cloth, and unusual foods and spices.

LOCATION: Great Zimbabwe, which means "great stone house," was sited on a high plateau in South Central Africa in Masvingo Province, Zimbabwe.

WHO LIVED HERE? The Shona of Zimbabwe were miners, farmers, cattle- and goat-herders, and spoke a language called Bantu. Seeking to escape disease-carrying tsetse flies in swampy lower elevations, they first settled Great Zimbabwe in the fourth century. By the eleventh century the Shona began building a village made of stone, which grew into a city of about fifteen thousand people.

WHY WAS IT LOST? Years of constant farming that made the soil less fertile, water shortages due to climatic changes, along with the depletion of nearby gold mines ended a long period of prosperity. After more than a thou-

sand years of existence, Great Zimbabwe was abandoned around 1450.

HOW WAS IT FOUND? German archaeologists discovered the surviving stone buildings and, because of their monumental appearance, assumed Arabians or Europeans had built them. Decades of research prove that Great Zimbabwe was indeed built by the African Shona who had expertly fitted the granite blocks together without mortar by using innovative iron tools.

WHAT'S MYSTERIOUS? What did the eight soapstone statues of birds with their human lips and toes represent? Were they monuments to the kings of Great Zimbabwe or depictions of the eagles that flew high above? Today, they are a symbol of Zimbabwe, and one of the birds adorns the country's flag.

ANGKOR WAT

If you had lived in this city, a vast collection of temples, houses, and monuments, you would have encountered bizarre creatures, such as monkey-like wild macaques and flying wingless snakes, as well as people perched on elephants or dressed in colored silk sarongs visiting the temples. Countless realistic stone sculptures of gods and animals would have made the walls of the temples seem teeming with life, making your sacred city a magical world both scary and exciting.

LOCATION: On the northwest shore of Tonlé Sap Lake, near the Mekong River delta, Cambodia

WHO LIVED HERE? The Khmer (kuh-mare) people inhabited this part of Asia for nearly four thousand years and established this Hindu temple complex in the beginning of the twelfth century. It took about three hundred thousand people and over six thousand elephants to build Angkor Wat, which became the largest religious complex in the world—bigger even than Karnak in Egypt. Dedicated to the Hindu god Vishnu who is believed to reside in the Himalayas, the towering temples symbolized those mountains.

WHY WAS IT LOST? At the end of the thirteenth century the city converted from Hinduism to Buddhism, and after a Thai invasion in 1431, the Khmer were forced to abandon their city, which was largely forgotten and neglected for the next four hundred years.

HOW WAS IT FOUND? When visited by a French archaeologist in the 1860s, Angkor Wat was nearly impenetrable, completely overgrown by the jungle.

WHAT'S MYSTERIOUS? Optic imaging by modern drones has shown that more temples interspersed throughout the remains of Angkor Wat are still hidden within the jungle. Will this entire city someday be excavated to expose its secrets?

MESA VERDE

If this was your village of over six hundred cliff dwellings built under gigantic rock outcrops, you would have to scramble up a tall wooden ladder to get to your house made of sandstone blocks and wooden beams. From the tower of your home, you and your family could gaze at the stars and see the changing position of the moon to determine the best time to plant garden crops.

LOCATION: Mesa Verde (Spanish for "green table") is in Colorado, USA.

WHO LIVED HERE? Nomadic or wandering Paleo-Indian tribes first inhabited Mesa Verde around 7500 BCE. Pueblo Indians arrived around 600 CE to settle permanently, and began to build the first pueblo-style dwellings near the steep cliffs that gave protection from harsh weather and invasions. Eventually, these Pueblo Indians burrowed their shelters deep within the clefts of the cliffs, giving them even more protection. Famous for their building skills, the Pueblos also wove baskets and made pottery, which is preserved in museums today.

WHY WAS IT LOST? After only about a century of habitation, the cliff dwellings at Mesa Verde were abandoned. No one knows why, but a factor may have been the difficulty of growing crops in such an arid climate with bitter cold winters and scorching summers. A growing population demanded an increasing food supply, and scholars believe the Pueblos moved to other locations that had milder climates and more dependable water sources. Today, you can visit the Mesa Verde site, including Cliff Palace with its two hundred rooms and twenty-three kivas (meeting halls).

HOW WAS IT FOUND? Four centuries after they were abandoned, the cliff dwellings at Mesa Verde were rediscovered by American explorers of the West. Mesa Verde became a protected archaeological site and a national park.

WHAT'S MYSTERIOUS? When the Pueblos abandoned their spectacular cliff dwellings after only a century, why did they leave many of their belongings behind as if they were going to return?

RAPA NUI or EASTER ISLAND

If you lived on this remote tropical island more than a thousand miles from land, your mother or father might have been one of the carvers who helped sculpt the nearly one thousand massive figures that dominate the landscape. Facing inland from the surrounding sea, these stone figures, called moai (mo-ai), meaning "living faces," have eyes inlaid with bright coral and seem to watch over the villages—except for eight that stand sentinel-like, looking out over the rough sea.

LOCATION: A territory of Chile, Rapa Nui (rap-a NOO-EE), now called Easter Island, is a remote speck in the Pacific Ocean, two thousand miles from Chile and over a thousand miles away from the closest inhabited island.

WHO LIVED HERE? Today's inhabitants are descendants of the Rapa Nui, a native Polynesian people who discovered Easter Island between 700 and 1100 CE after paddling hand-crafted double-hulled canoes from distant island to distant island over the vast Pacific.

WHY WAS IT LOST? After peaking at about fifteen thousand people in the 1600s, the population declined drastically due to the island's isolation, erosion of soil, and loss of trees that once provided wood for house and boat building. Raids, exploitation by foreign

explorers, and the introduction of diseases also diminished the population to such an extent that the reasons for erecting the moai were forgotten.

HOW WAS IT FOUND? Because Easter Island has no natural harbor and the surf is rough, arrival by ship was extremely treacherous, and visits were therefore infrequent. The first recorded European sighting occurred on Easter Sunday in 1722 by a Dutch explorer who renamed the island of Rapa Nui after a brief stay.

WHAT'S MYSTERIOUS? Exactly why were the moai created? Whom do they represent? Because of their size and weight, from fifteen to as much as three hundred tons—heavier than a train engine—how were they moved from the quarry and placed miles away across the island?

TENOCHTITLÁN

What would it be like to live in a vast city that seemed to float on a lake? Here roads on dikes and bridges led to canals where you could paddle your dugout canoe past palaces and pyramids topped with temples built to honor your Aztec gods. Atop the largest pyramid were two temples, built side by side—one for the hummingbird god and the other for the rain god.

LOCATION: Tenochtitlán (teh-notch-TIT-lahn), or "the cactus," was constructed in the shallow Lake Texcoco, in what is now the center of Mexico City.

WHO LIVED HERE? When searching for a place to build a city in 1325, an Aztec tribe called the Mexica chose the site after seeing an eagle perched on a cactus devouring a snake—an omen that this was their home. Ferocious warriors, the Mexica also farmed on floating gardens, fished from canoes with nets and spears, wrote histories called codices, and, with their skills in astronomy, developed a 365-day calendar. They built enormous stepped pyramids, which housed temples, although religious ceremonies in these temples were often cruel, with both human and animal sacrifices.

WHY WAS IT LOST? By about 1500, Tenochtitlán, the capital of the Aztec Empire, was the largest city in pre-Columbian America, with more than two hundred thousand people. But during the Spanish conquest of the Aztecs in 1519, Hernán Cortés largely destroyed the city, and an enormous Christian cathedral was built over the Aztec ruins as the center of their New World empire.

HOW WAS IT FOUND? Ruins of the main temple were rediscovered in the Zócalo square, at the center of Mexico City, in the early twentieth century. Major excavations have continued, and, as recently as 2017, an unusual circular Aztec temple and ball court were discovered.

WHAT'S MYSTERIOUS? The elaborate architecture of Tenochtitlán was unknown to the rest of the world until the Spaniards arrived. Yet, it had many similarities to the European and Mediterranean style: pyramids rivaling those of Egypt, city gates, busy squares and marketplaces, and palaces as grand as those in the cities of Spain. To this day, it remains a mystery that two civilizations totally unknown to each other, the Western culture of Europe and the Mediterranean and that of the Aztecs, would have both developed such similar monumental architecture.

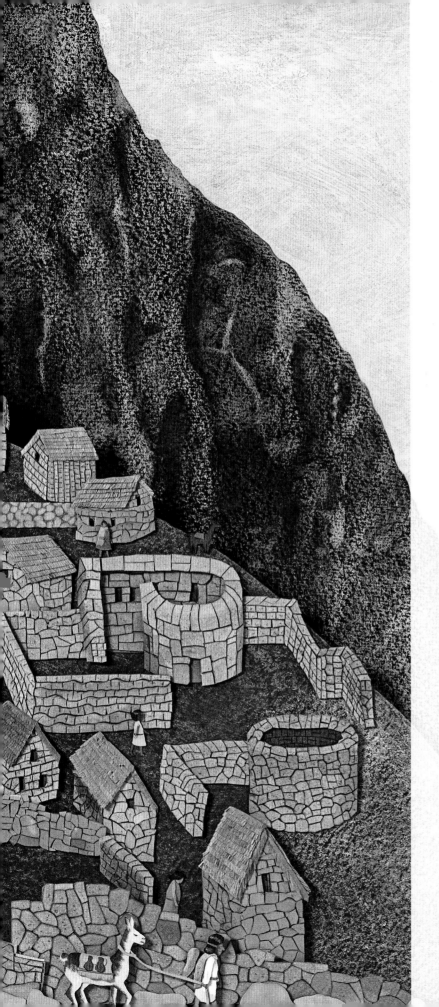

MACHU PICCHU

How would you like to live high in the clouds in a city perched on mountain terraces? Here you could ride your family's llama on granite stairways past fountains filled with water flowing down from stone aqueducts, and for your dinner teams of runners would bring fresh fish from the Pacific Ocean hundreds of miles away.

LOCATION: The mile-and-a-half-high site of Machu Picchu (ma-choo PICK-choo) is located between two peaks of the Andes Mountains in Peru.

WHO LIVED HERE? Beginning as a small tribe near Cuzco, Peru, in the twelfth century, the Inca grew, in just a few hundred years, into a vast empire, stretching thousands of miles along the South American Pacific coast and connected by stone-paved roads to the capital in Cuzco—although the Inca had no wheeled vehicles! In 1438 the emperor ordered the construction of a royal estate for his family on top of Machu Picchu to be closer to the sun god. Ruling from this remote retreat in the sky, they lived in the largest house while his servants, cooks, gardeners, and craftsmen lived in smaller houses nearby.

WHY WAS IT LOST? Incan stone weapons were no match against Spanish gunpowder, armor, and horses, and with the capture of their emperor, the Inca Empire quickly col-

lapsed—so swiftly that the Spaniards never discovered the distant and ultimately abandoned Machu Picchu.

HOW WAS IT FOUND? In 1911 the American explorer Hiram Bingham climbed Machu Picchu on a steep jungle path in search of a rumored "lost city." When nearing the top, he shared lunch with a family who farmed on ancient stone terraces, and the farmer asked his eight-year-old son, Pablito, to guide Bingham to the summit. After ascending terrace after terrace, like climbing a giant's stone stairs, Bingham was amazed to see before him buildings made of irregular stones that fit together like pieces of an enormous jigsaw puzzle.

WHAT'S MYSTERIOUS? The Inca's massive building stones tightly interlock without mortar, so that in the event of earth tremors the stones only jostle and then fall perfectly back into place. How did the Inca achieve such precision without metal tools?

FATEHPUR SIKRI

If you had visited this fanciful city, the capital of a vast empire, you might have shopped in colorful marketplaces called bazaars, attended the Great Mosque, or enjoyed cooling breezes in the Wind Tower before stopping for a rest in the Dream House. Magnificent gates protected and allowed entry into the city, including the Elephant Gate, with column capitals in the form of elephant heads, and the Drum House gate, where an imperial band played festive music to welcome important visitors.

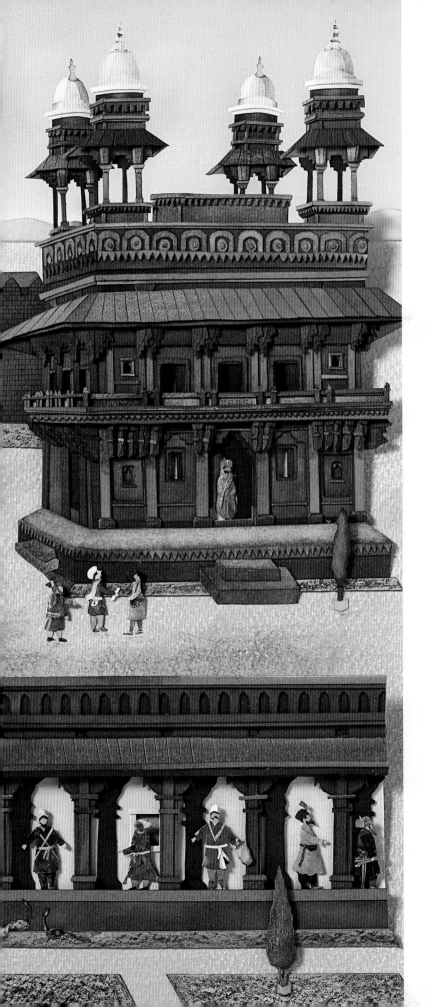

LOCATION: Fatehpur Sikri (fa-tay-puur see-kree) is in a state in north central India called Uttar Pradesh.

WHO LIVED HERE? Between 1569 and 1571, King Akbar, a Mughal (moh-guhl), built the city in honor of a Sufi saint who prophesized that the king would have a son. Akbar named it Fatehpur Sikri, "city of victory." Although it served as the Mughal capital, it was to last for less than two decades.

WHY WAS IT LOST? A spring-fed lake that provided water for Fatehpur dried up as the population grew, and as a result the capital was moved in 1585 to Lahore, a city in what is now Pakistan.

HOW WAS IT FOUND? In 1899 Englishman Lord Curzon, viceroy of India during the British occupation and famed for his role in restoring the nearby magnificent Taj Mahal, visited the abandoned red sandstone buildings of Fatehpur and ordered their preservation.

WHAT'S MYSTERIOUS? There was almost always something fun and unusual going on in Fatehpur. One of the city squares is mysteriously patterned like a life-size board for the king's favorite game, Pachisi. Were members of the king's royal household and citizens of Fatehpur asked to dress in colorful costumes to become the game pieces and move in a process of removal until only one person was left standing?

JAMESTOWN

To have lived in this stockaded and fortified village, you would have left your home to sail with your father on a five-month voyage across the ocean to seek a better life in an unknown land. As you helped build your new home, you would have discovered that other people already lived in this land, spoke a different language, and had lives completely unlike your own.

LOCATION: Jamestown colony was settled on May 4, 1607, on a peninsula in the James River near the Powhatan Indian Confederacy in what is now the state of Virginia.

WHO LIVED HERE? Despite the failure of earlier colonies, over one hundred men and boys sponsored by King James I left England in 1606 on three ships bound for the new world of America, determined to build a permanent home. Jamestown also nearly failed, but conditions improved under the leadership of Captain John Smith and with the assistance of Powhatan, the Native American chief and father of Pocahontas, who later married one of the colonists. With the building of homes, a church, and a fort, Jamestown became the first permanent English settlement in the New World and the first of the thirteen original colonies that were to become the first thirteen states of the USA in 1776.

WHY WAS IT LOST? The chosen site proved to be marshy, unsuitable for farming, and unable to sustain a growing population. After the capital moved to Williamsburg, Jamestown reverted to fields and was forgotten, thought to have been washed away by the James River.

HOW WAS IT FOUND? After extensive study of the site in 1994, the archaeologist William Kelso believed the fort site still existed but lay buried on the riverside, and began excavations. The first shovelfuls unearthed artifacts, such as glass trade beads, rings, coins, thimbles, and scissors, and numerous house foundations. Even skeletons of the colonists have since been uncovered. Some of these colonists have been identified and, through digital imaging, pictures of their appearances have been created.

WHAT'S MYSTERIOUS? Relationships between the colonists and the Native Americans were not always friendly, although it is recorded that several Jamestown boys, for unknown reasons, went to live with the Powhatans. After learning their language and survival skills, they were sometimes surprisingly able to reconcile the two groups.

CAUGHNAWAGA

If you had lived in this village of houses made entirely of tree trunks and bark, you would have shared one long room with as many as a dozen families. Your family would have been skilled at bending young birch tree saplings to form the framework of your longhouse, which was then clad with strips of elm tree bark. A wall made of the same materials, called a palisade, surrounded the longhouses and would have protected your family from invading tribes and wild animals. Longhouses could easily be enlarged to accommodate growing families, and some were as long as 335 feet—longer than a football field.

LOCATION: Caughnawaga (kag-na-waga) is on the banks of the Mohawk River in what is now upstate New York.

WHO LIVED HERE? The Iroquois (ee-ro-kwoi) called themselves Haudenosaunee (howd-en-saw-nee), or "people of the longhouse," and lived in the northeast woodlands between the Atlantic coast and the Mississippi River. A tribe of the Iroquois known as Mohawks constructed this village of twelve longhouses around 1670 in a wild mountainous area near the whitewater rapids of the Mohawk River. They were hunters, but they also grew corn, beans, and squash, and used the river as a trading route with other tribes and the English colonists. Each longhouse was governed by the eldest mother of the residing families.

WHY WAS IT LOST? As the invasive French and English colonization pushed west, the Mohawks joined four other tribes to form the Iroquois League, an alliance that was ultimately defeated, forcing the Mohawks to abandon their villages in the east and form new ones in Wisconsin, Oklahoma, and Canada.

HOW WAS IT FOUND? In 1950 evidence of the stockade walls and outlines of the longhouses were found. Today, Caughnawaga has been excavated and rebuilt and has the largest collection of longhouses in North America.

WHAT'S MYSTERIOUS? The doors of each longhouse were made of animal hide or hinged sheets of bark, and above each front door was a carved animal symbol, such as a turtle, beaver, bear, rabbit, or bird. Were these symbols meant to represent the names of each longhouse?

TIMELINE

KARNAK ca. 3100 BCE
First monuments are built

BABYLON ca. 2350 BCE
Small village on the Euphrates
River is settled

AKROTIRI ca. 2200 BCE
Is settled

HERCULANEUM ca. 600 BCE
Is founded

GREAT ZIMBABWE ca. 1000
Construction of stone village
begins

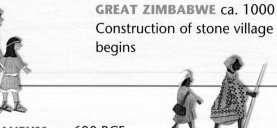

ANGKOR WAT ca. 1100
Construction begins by
the Khmer

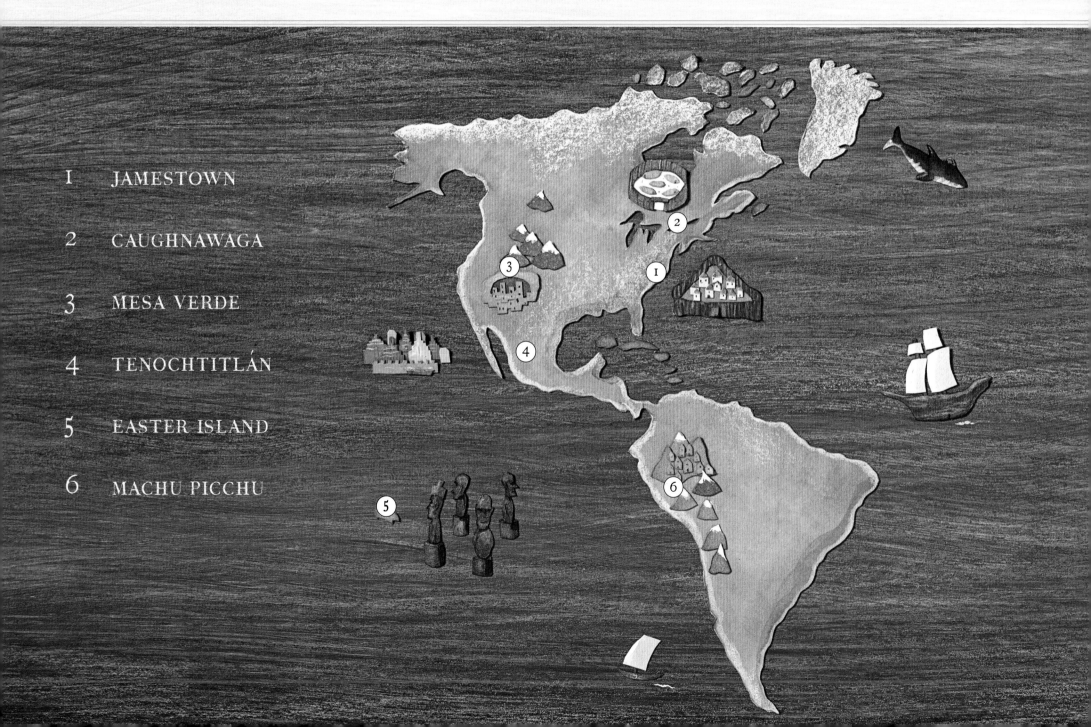

1   JAMESTOWN

2   CAUGHNAWAGA

3   MESA VERDE

4   TENOCHTITLÁN

5   EASTER ISLAND

6   MACHU PICCHU

MESA VERDE ca. late 1100s
First cliff dwellings are built

TENOCHTITLÁN 1325
Site is chosen

FATEHPUR SIKRI 1569–1571
City is built

CAUGHNAWAGA ca. 1670
Mohawk village is established

EASTER ISLAND ca. 700–1100
Is settled

MACHU PICCHU 1438
Construction begins
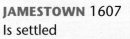

JAMESTOWN 1607
Is settled

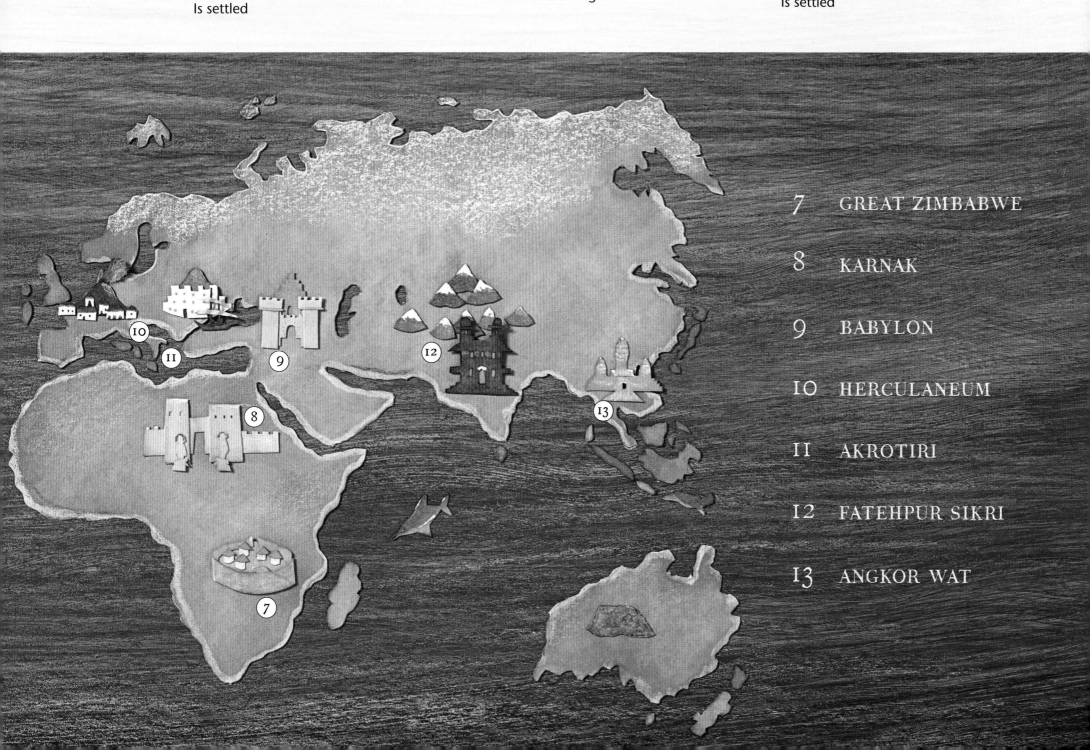

7   GREAT ZIMBABWE

8   KARNAK

9   BABYLON

10   HERCULANEUM

11   AKROTIRI

12   FATEHPUR SIKRI

13   ANGKOR WAT

A NOTE ON THE ARTWORK

Each illustration for this book involves many stages of cutting, painting, and gluing up to seven or eight layers of paper within each image. The spacing between each layer creates shadows to give the illustration a visible dimensional quality. For publication, they are professionally photographed with special lighting effects to enhance the dramatic impact.

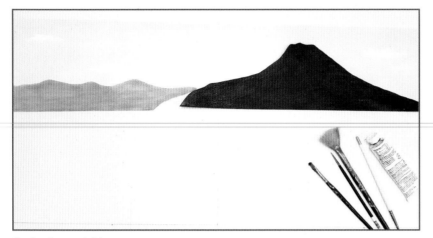

1: Background layers

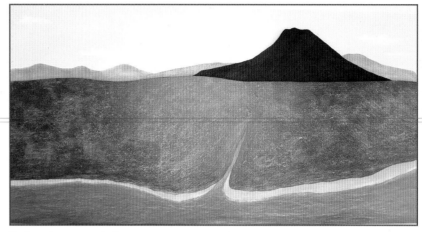

2: Landscape painting

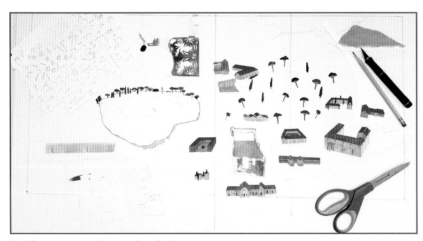

3: Element cutting and coloring

4: Careful placement

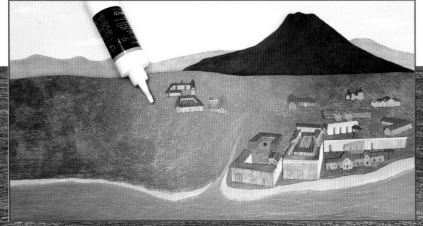

5: Glue time

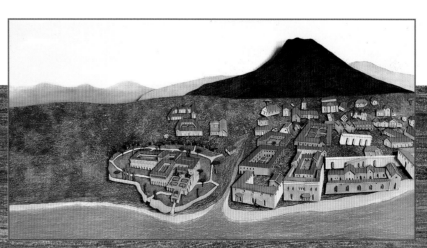

6: Final touches!

SELECTED SOURCES

Adam, Simon. *Kingfisher Atlas of World History*. New York: Kingfisher, 2010.

Adams, Mark. *Turn Right at Machu Picchu: Rediscovering the Lost City One Step at a Time*. New York: Dutton, 2011.

Ambler, Richard. *The Anasazi*. Flagstaff, AZ: Museum of Northern Arizona, 1977.

Coe, Michael, Dean Snow, and Elizabeth Benson. *Atlas of Ancient America*. New York, Facts On File, 1986.

Crump, Donald J., ed. *Splendors of the Past: Lost Cities of the Ancient World*. Washington, DC: National Geographic Press, 1981.

Deiss, Joseph Jay. *Herculaneum: Italy's Buried Treasure*. Malibu, CA: J. Paul Getty Museum Press, 1989.

Garlake, Peter. *The Making of the Past: The Kingdoms of Africa*. New York: Peter Bedrick Books, 1990.

Harper, James, and Jennifer Westwood. *Atlas of Legendary Places*. New York: Grove Press, 1989.

Kelso, William, M. *Jamestown: The Buried Truth*. Charlottesville, VA: University of Virginia Press, 2006.

Lange, Kurt, and Max Hirmer. *Egypt: Architecture, Sculpture, Painting, in Three Thousand Years*. London: Phaidon, 1956.

Lloyd, Seton, Hans Wolfgang Müller, and Roland Martin. *Ancient Architecture: Mesopotamia, Egypt, Crete, Greece*. New York: Abrams, 1972.

Roveda, Vittorio. *Sacred Angkor: The Carved Reliefs of Angkor Wat*. Bangkok: River Books, 2003.

Scarre, Dr. Chris, ed. *Past Worlds: Atlas of Archaeology*. Ann Arbor, MI: Borders Books in association with HarperCollins, 2003. First published by Times Books, 1988.

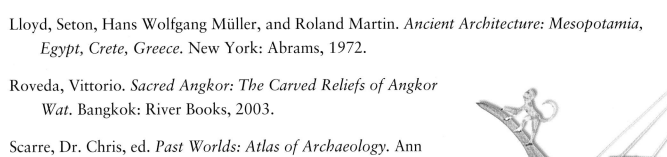